TECHNICAL
R E P O R T

An Overview of Past Proposals for Military Retirement Reform

John Christian

Prepared for the Office of the Secretary of Defense

NATIONAL DEFENSE RESEARCH INSTITUTE

The research described in this report was prepared for the Office of the Secretary of Defense (OSD). The research was conducted in the RAND National Defense Research Institute, a federally funded research and development center sponsored by the Office of the Secretary of Defense, the Joint Staff, the Unified Combatant Commands, the Department of the Navy, the Marine Corps, the defense agencies, and the defense Intelligence Community under Contract DASW01-01-C-0004.

Library of Congress Cataloging-in-Publication Data

Christian, John, 1971–
    An overview of past programs for military retirement reform / John Christian.
      p. cm.
    "TR-376."
    Includes bibliographical references.
    ISBN-13: 978-0-8330-3987-3 (pbk. : alk. paper)
    1. United States—Armed Forces—Appointments and retirements—History. I. Title.

UB443.C47 2006
331.25'29135500973—dc22

2006024151

The RAND Corporation is a nonprofit research organization providing objective analysis and effective solutions that address the challenges facing the public and private sectors around the world. RAND's publications do not necessarily reflect the opinions of its research clients and sponsors.

RAND® is a registered trademark.

Published 2006 by the RAND Corporation
1776 Main Street, P.O. Box 2138, Santa Monica, CA 90407-2138
1200 South Hayes Street, Arlington, VA 22202-5050
4570 Fifth Avenue, Suite 600, Pittsburgh, PA 15213
RAND URL: http://www.rand.org/
To order RAND documents or to obtain additional information, contact
Distribution Services: Telephone: (310) 451-7002;
Fax: (310) 451-6915; Email: order@rand.org

Preface

The Department of Defense has sought to identify military retirement plan alternatives for active and reserve personnel that will have desired features of force management flexibility, comparability to civilian-sector retirement, and cost-effectiveness.

This technical report was originally written as a project memorandum entailing a review of past studies of retirement. It is intended to give the Department of Defense background and insight into previous research on military retirement, so that it might be possible to learn from and build upon past reform proposals and apply those insights to new alternatives. The report covers the last 60 years of military retirement studies, beginning at the time when the key components of the current retirement plan were crystallizing. Most reform proposals have focused on the regular retirement system; this document reflects that emphasis but also includes a description of reserve retirement proposals. This report is written for a broad policy audience.

In addition to this technical report, two other RAND Corporation documents are associated with this research: Beth Asch, James Hosek, and David Loughran, *Reserve Retirement Reform: A Viewpoint on Recent Congressional Proposals,* TR-199-OSD, Santa Monica, Calif.: RAND Corporation, 2006; Beth Asch and Daniel Clendenning, unpublished RAND research on a policy analysis of reserve retirement reform.

This research was sponsored by the Office of the Under Secretary of Defense for Personnel and Readiness and conducted within the Forces and Resources Policy Center of the RAND National Defense Research Institute, a federally funded research and development center sponsored by the Office of the Secretary of Defense, the Joint Staff, the Unified Combatant Commands, the Department of the Navy, the Marine Corps, the defense agencies, and the defense Intelligence Community.

For more information on RAND's Forces and Resources Policy Center, contact the Director, James Hosek. He can be reached by e-mail at James_Hosek@rand.org; by phone at 310-393-0411, extension 7183; or by mail at the RAND Corporation, 1776 Main Street, Santa Monica, California 90407-2138. More information about RAND is available at www.rand.org.

Contents

Preface iii

Tables vii

Summary ix

Abbreviations xi

An Overview of Past Proposals for Military Retirement Reform 1

Current Military Retirement System Provisions 1

Military Retirement Before World War II 2

Cost 4

Equity 8

Selective Retention 10

Civilian Comparability 11

Force Management Flexibility 13

Reserve Retirement Reform 15

Conclusion 19

Bibliography 21

Tables

1. Comparison of Retirement Reform Proposals... 16
2. Sixth QRMC Reserve Retirement Alternatives 18

Summary

This technical report provides an overview of the history of U.S. military retirement studies and associated legislation, with a particular focus on the past 60 years of proposed reforms. The emphasis is on regular (as opposed to reserve) nondisability retirement because of the relative weight that reformers have placed on the regular retirement system. It is organized around the following five major issues that have driven attempts at retirement system reform:

- *Cost:* Reducing the benefits associated with the transition from active duty to civilian life during the so-called "second-career phase" of military retirement. (The term "second-career phase" refers to the fact that service members who are fully vested receive an immediate annuity upon retirement, which is often at a young enough age for them to embark on a second career until they reach old-age retirement.)
- *Equity:* Providing benefits for members separating before 20 years of service (YOS) as well as for those who are vested at 20 YOS.
- *Selective retention:* Increasing incentives for key service members to stay beyond 20 YOS.
- *Civilian comparability:* Providing a defined contribution plan that vests earlier than 20 YOS. (The military retirement system is a defined benefit plan, commonly called a pension plan in the private sector. The Thrift Savings Plan is a type of defined contribution plan.[1])
- *Force management flexibility:* Providing tools for the services to create variable career lengths when needed for force management.

To provide context, this report begins with a brief overview of the current provisions (e.g., vesting rules and benefit formulas) of the regular and reserve retirement systems before going into detail about the history of reform efforts. It also includes a brief commentary on reforms aimed at the reserve retirement system as a point of comparison.

---

[1] A defined benefit plan is characterized by mandatory participation and strict benefit formulas based on YOS and pay. A defined contribution plan is characterized by voluntary participation and benefits that are based on the amounts that participants and employers contribute to the plan plus interest income. For a discussion of the differences between the military's pension system and the Thrift Savings Plan, see U.S. Department of Defense, 2005, p. 939.

Abbreviations

CPI	Consumer Price Index
DMC	Defense Manpower Commission
DoD	Department of Defense
DSB	Defense Science Board Task Force on Human Resource Strategy
ERISA	Employee Retirement Income Security Act
IAC	Interagency Committee on Uniformed Services Retirement and Survivor Benefits
MRRA	Military Retirement Reform Act of 1986 (also known as REDUX)
PCMC	President's Commission on Military Compensation (Zwick Commission)
QRMC	Quadrennial Review of Military Compensation
RCSS	Reserve Compensation System Study of 1978
REDUX	See MRRA
RMA	Retirement Modernization Act of 1974
TSP	Thrift Savings Plan
USRBA	Uniformed Services Retirement Benefits Act
YOS	years of service

An Overview of Past Proposals for Military Retirement Reform

Current Military Retirement System Provisions

As of the writing of this report (2003), there are three regular retirement formulas and two reserve retirement formulas in use. In both retirement systems, the formula that applies to a service member depends on the member's date of entry into military service. This section discusses the current regular retirement provisions, followed by the current reserve retirement provisions.

In the regular retirement system, for persons who entered service before September 8, 1980, retirement pay is calculated as 2.5 percent per year of service times the final rate of monthly basic pay. For persons who entered service from September 8, 1980, through July 31, 1986, or persons who entered after July 31, 1986, and did not accept a 15-year Career Status Bonus, retirement pay is calculated as 2.5 percent per year of service times the average monthly basic pay rate for the member's highest 36 months of basic pay. The final regular retirement formula in use applies to persons who entered service after July 31, 1986, and accepted a 15-year Career Status Bonus with an additional 5-year service obligation; retirement pay for these persons is calculated as 2.5 percent per year of service, less one percentage point for each year of service completed less than 30 years, to a maximum of 75 percent, times average monthly basic pay for the highest 36 months of basic pay.[1] These persons also receive a $30,000 Career Status Bonus at 15 years of service (YOS) and also have their retirement multiplier (i.e., 2.5 percent times YOS) restored to its full amount when they reach age 62. Cost-of-living adjustments are equal to the Consumer Price Index (CPI) minus 1 percent until age 62, when there is a one-time, full CPI restoration of purchasing power, followed by CPI minus 1 percent increases thereafter. For all three of these formulas, a service member becomes vested after 20 YOS. The annuity is payable immediately upon retirement regardless of age.

The reserve retirement system uses a "point" system to determine YOS. Using this process, a person qualifies for reserve retired pay upon completion of 20 years of "satisfactory federal service" as a member of the Armed Forces.[2] Satisfactory federal service is defined as an anniversary year in which at least 50 retirement credit points are awarded. A reservist earns

---

[1] The REDUX formula can be stated verbally in many different ways, but all formulations reduce to the expression $0.035 \times YOS - 0.3$.

[2] Originally, the last eight YOS had to be in a reserve component for the person to qualify for reserve retirement pay. This minimum requirement was first reduced in 2003 and then eliminated entirely in 2005.

one "active-duty" point for each day of active duty or active-duty training; he or she earns one "inactive-duty" point for attendance at a unit training assembly, typically two points per weekend drill day. A reservist automatically receives 15 inactive-duty points for each year he or she is a member of a reserve component; he or she may also receive inactive-duty points for completion of accredited courses. The difference between active- and inactive-duty points is that there is no upper limit on active-duty points that can be earned in a year, whereas inactive-duty points are capped at 90. One of two reserve retirement formulas is then used to compute retirement pay. For persons who entered service before September 8, 1980, retirement pay is calculated by (1) dividing the person's total points (active and inactive) by 360 to convert the points into years of satisfactory federal service,[3] (2) taking the monthly basic pay rate for the member's grade and length of service at the time the member becomes entitled to retired pay at age 60, (3) multiplying that pay rate by 2.5 percent per year of service credited under the point system, and (4) subtracting any excess over 75 percent of the pay basis. For persons who join the military on or after September 8, 1980, the formula is the same, but the pay basis is different. For these persons, the pay basis is the average of the monthly basic pay to which the member would have been entitled had he or she been on active duty for the last three years he or she was a member of the reserves.

Military Retirement Before World War II

Before describing the more recent efforts at retirement system reform, it is useful to provide a brief description of the origins of the military retirement system and its history up to the point of World War II, roughly when the current retirement system took shape.

U.S. military retirement can trace its roots to a statute in 1855 that gave the Secretary of the Navy the right, with the recommendation of an examination board, to involuntarily terminate officers who were deemed incapable or unfit for duty. Before 1855 there existed no legislative authority for such actions. Officers removed from active duty under this law were placed on a "reserve list" and entitled to half their pay, unless they were deemed culpable for their incapacity (U.S. Department of Defense, 2005, p. 685). Six years later, legislation authorized voluntary retirement of all officers of all services after 40 YOS. The impetus for these reforms and others like them during this era was the preservation of a "young and vigorous" officer corps.

Subsequent legislation reduced the YOS required to become eligible for voluntary retirement. In 1870, Army and Marine Corps officers became eligible for retirement after 30 YOS. This regulation was extended to Navy officers in 1908. In 1935, voluntary retirement for Army officers was established at 15 YOS; this level was the fewest YOS ever required for voluntary

---

[3]   A reservist can obviously receive slightly more than one year of creditable service per calendar year using this formula; in addition, the reserve retirement point system allows for fractions of YOS, whereas the regular retirement system allows for fractions of YOS only for the final year of active duty.

military retirement. The current system of vesting at 20 YOS began in 1946 for Navy and Marine Corps officers and in 1948 for officers of the Army and the newly established Air Force.

The first legislative authority for voluntary retirement of enlisted personnel came in 1885, when Army and Marine enlisted personnel could retire after 30 YOS. Until that point, the superannuation problem was only a concern with officers. Policymakers believed that the "youth and vigor" of the enlisted ranks could be maintained effectively with selective reenlistment management (U.S. Department of Defense, 2005, p. 695). Eventually the services decided that the same retirement benefits extended to officers should be extended to enlisted personnel as well, for reasons of private-sector competitiveness and the welfare of service members. By 1945, the enlisted personnel of all the services became eligible for voluntary retirement at 20 YOS. Thus, by roughly the middle of the 20th century, all U.S. military service members—enlisted and officers—became vested in a retirement benefit after 20 YOS.

Vesting provisions are not the only retirement plan features that bear historical explication. The current retirement pay formulas have their origins in the earliest Navy officer retirement legislation from 1855. That legislation produced a "leave of absence" pay for separated Navy officers at the rate of 75 percent of sea duty pay. In comparison, Army and Marine Corps officers were entitled to retired pay in the amount of their "pay proper" plus four rations, in accordance with an 1862 law. When the armed forces transitioned from pay and rations to a salary system in 1871, Army and Marine Corps officers began to receive a retirement benefit equal to 75 percent of their base and longevity pay. In 1916, the military established its "up-or-out" promotion system and also settled on the "standard" retirement pay formula of 2.5 percent times YOS, up to a maximum of 75 percent. This formula has remained largely unchanged since that time.

Several conclusions emerge from this brief overview of the origins of the military retirement. The first conclusion is that the current provisions of the retirement system have deep antecedents in the legislative history of the armed forces; vesting rules and payout formulas have similarities to some program components of the late 1800s. The second conclusion is that the genesis of these provisions lies primarily in the need for military personnel who are not diminished by old age. Over time, additional personnel and force management objectives have gained in importance, and the tradition and history of the military retirement system have often been at odds with these new goals.[4]

We turn now to the past 60 years of military retirement reform, focusing separately on each of the five, major objectives of these reforms: cost, equity, selective retention, civilian comparability, and force management flexibility.

---

[4] Although the advancement of a "youthful and vigorous" force has long been the primary goal of the retirement system, other objectives that mirror today's concerns were evident early on. For example, the Navy instituted a voluntary early retirement option in 1899 to improve officer promotion opportunities and to maintain the flow of officers into the lieutenant commander through captain ranks. See U.S. Department of Defense, 2005, p. 687.

Cost

The objectives of military retirement reform studies share some common themes. Foremost among the concerns of the commissions and study groups is the effect of retirement pay on force structure and readiness. However, concerns about the cost of the retirement system have been a major focus of previous policymakers. Because of the large number of armed services retirees, small changes to the retirement formula can have a profound effect on cost. To some extent, the desire among policymakers to reduce the cost of the system has fluctuated with economic conditions. Cost reduction proposals surfaced as early as the 1948 Advisory Commission on Service Pay (also known as the Hook Commission). The Hook Commission instituted many of the military compensation reforms that exist today, such as the pay and allowances system. On military retirement, the commission stated that the benefit should be delivered at minimum cost (Advisory Commission on Service Pay, 1948, p. 41). Because a service member with 20 YOS could retire typically at age 42 with half of his or her basic pay, the retirement system was seen as overly liberal. The Hook Commission recommended changing the system so that a person could retire after 30 YOS at any age, or after 20 YOS only if the member had attained age 60 (for officers) or age 50 (for enlisted personnel).

The Joint Army-Navy Pay Board roughly coincided with the Hook Commission. On the issue of cost, the joint pay board proposed that the retirement annuity be delayed, payable at age 62 (Asch and Warner, 1994b, p. 29).

The next major study of military retirement came in 1969 with the establishment of the Quadrennial Review of Military Compensation (QRMC). To lower the cost of the retirement system, the first QRMC developed a distinction between an old-age phase and a second-career phase of retirement. The 20-year vesting rule and immediate annuity payments made a second-career phase viable for many military retirees, and the first QRMC proposed lower retired pay during the second-career phase than during the phase when the retiree is out of the labor force entirely. In the view of the review committee, the retirement system subsidized retirees too generously during the second-career phase, when all that was warranted was a benefit equal to the second-career earnings loss associated with transition to the civilian labor force. For the period from separation to full retirement age—the second-career phase—the first QRMC proposed a benefit equal to 24 percent of final salary at 20 YOS up to 51 percent of final salary at 30 YOS. The old-age annuity would range from 33 percent of final salary at 20 YOS to 75 percent of final salary at 40 YOS.

In 1971, the Interagency Committee on Uniformed Services Retirement and Survivor Benefits (IAC) followed the first QRMC report. IAC reviewed the recommendations of the first QRMC and developed a new set of recommendations. IAC also suggested a two-tier retirement system, with different second-career and old-age annuity benefit levels. During the first-tier (second-career) phase, retirees would receive a 2 percent reduction per year of service under age 60 (for those separating after 20–24 YOS), or a 2 percent reduction per year of service under age 55 (for those separating after 25 YOS). The full annuity would be paid at ages 60 and 55, respectively, in conjunction with the start of the second-tier (old-age) phase. The IAC proposal broke new ground by arguing for the use of an individual's highest three years of average basic pay, rather than the final basic pay used in the prevailing benefit calculation. Such a change would generally lower the cost of retirement benefit payments, since an individual's average final three years of basic pay is typically less than his or her basic pay rate at separation.

The IAC and the Department of Defense (DoD) Retirement Study Group led to the Uniformed Services Retirement Modernization Act of 1974 (RMA, H.R. 12505). The reduction of retirement costs was one of the stated objectives of the RMA, and it proposed three major changes toward that end (U.S. Defense Manpower Commission, Vol. V, 1976, pp. 1, 53). First, the RMA proposed a high-one pay base (i.e., average annual basic pay in the highest year before separation) for calculating retirement benefits. The averaging method was a departure from the prevailing system of using the highest level of basic pay, which had the potential for last-minute increases. Such a change would lower costs somewhat, but it was not as great a change as that proposed by the IAC. Second, the RMA proposed a flat 15 percentage point reduction in the first-tier (second-career) annuity amount from the time of separation until 30 YOS would have been completed by the individual, at which point the full annuity amount would be restored. For example, under the prevailing plan, at 20 YOS the retiree would have received 50 percent of final pay, but under the RMA he or she would receive 35 percent of final average pay—a 15 percent reduction. Third, the RMA also included a plan to integrate military retirement and Social Security benefits. Under the prevailing system, the two annuities were additive. The RMA proposed an offset that reduced the military annuity by 50 percent of the amount of the Social Security benefit attributable to military service.

Following the RMA, which was *not* enacted, the Defense Manpower Commission (DMC) in 1976 also sought to reduce overall retirement costs. There were several components of the DMC proposal that were intended to achieve this goal. Like the IAC, the DMC recommended the use of the average of the highest three years of basic pay instead of final basic pay. In addition, the DMC proposed a reduction in benefit levels, as well as pushing back the start of annuity payments to age 65 (or a reduced annuity at age 60). On the issue of the Social Security offset, the DMC undertook a series of analyses and modeling exercises to assess the impact of that feature.[5] The DMC concluded that there was an "insoluble attribution problem" with the RMA's proposal; in other words, there was no way of unambiguously apportioning an individual's Social Security benefit to military service and to civilian employers.[6] The offset would deprive service members of income they would have received if they had never been eligible for Social Security benefits at all. Consequently, the DMC recommended scrapping the Social Security integration plan and argued against passage of the RMA as it stood.[7]

---

[5] The following example illustrates how the Social Security offset would work as provided in the RMA: A member retiring with $1,000 in military retired pay and $1,000 in Social Security benefits would have his or her military retired pay reduced ("offset") by 50 percent of the basic Social Security old-age benefit attributable to military service; so, in this example, if the member's Social Security benefit is 75 percent attributable to military service, his or her military retired pay would be reduced by 50 percent times 75 percent of $1,000, or $375.

[6] According to the study, this problem arises from the structure of the formula relating Social Security benefits to average earnings as well as the method of calculating average earnings. See U.S. Defense Manpower Commission, 1976, pp. 3–4.

[7] The DMC not only rejected the RMA proposal, but also the third QRMC's recommendations on retirement, which supported the RMA. See U.S. Department of Defense, 1996, p. 810.

The President's Commission on Military Compensation (PCMC, also known as the Zwick Commission) followed the DMC retirement study. Its report was issued in April 1978. Describing its overall philosophy, the PCMC stated that military compensation (including retired pay) should be "more cost-effective, flexible, and fair" (PCMC, 1978, p. 11). One of the primary concerns of the PCMC was the high cost of military compensation, which it said was becoming comparable with civilian salaries. It noted that military retirement costs had risen from 2 percent of the defense budget in 1964 to 8 percent of the budget in 1978—a result of the large standing force during the height of the Cold War that was just then retiring. As a result, the PCMC proposed annuity levels similar to those of the Federal Civil Service. It also revived the idea of a Social Security offset, opting for a partial integration plan. The DoD analyzed the PCMC proposal, and the outgrowth of this analysis was the Uniformed Services Retirement Benefits Act (USRBA) of 1979.[8]

On September 8, 1980, the National Defense Authorization Act of 1981 was enacted. The most significant change to military retirement from a cost reduction perspective was the move away from the use of final basic pay toward the use of the average of the highest three years of basic pay in the calculation of retiree benefits. The intent of this reform was to reduce what was then perceived as the rapidly increasing cost of military retirement (U.S. Department of Defense, 1996, p. 520). Because of the switch to an average pay value rather than straight final pay, future retirement payments would generally be lower and certain windfall benefits would be mitigated (e.g., a service member retiring immediately after a longevity increase or promotion). The legislation applied only to those service members enlisting on or after the date of enactment. At the time, this was the most significant legislative change to the military retirement system since the World War II era.

The fifth QRMC, the next major review of military retirement, issued its report in January 1984. The fifth QRMC did not propose a single retirement plan, but instead offered a range of alternative retirement reforms designed to meet various objectives. They included a reduced multiplier and a reduced cost of living adjustment. A Social Security offset was not recommended.

The fifth QRMC led to the enactment of the National Defense Authorization Act of 1984, which established a DoD Military Retirement Fund, under which military retirement costs were placed on an accrual accounting basis. This change added transparency to DoD budgeting by attaching an explicit cost to the future retirement pay liability of current-year personnel decisions. The intent was to ensure that military retirement was no longer a "pay-as-you-go," unfunded system.[9] Because of this accounting change, the pay and allowances costs (a set of compensation costs that includes basic pay, the housing allowance, etc.) of service members appear greater within the DoD budget than they would have been without the change.[10]

---

[8]   See the section of this report on civilian comparability for a discussion of USRBA.

[9]   The established fund is called the Department of Defense Military Retirement Fund.

[10]   There are indications that this accounting change, while useful for budgetary purposes, does not accurately reflect the true economic cost of a service member. The reason for the discrepancy is that DoD personnel cost accounting does not take into consideration the probability that an individual service member will retire from the military and thus receive his or her accrued benefit. The accrual charge, however, represents an accurate average cost per surviving service member.

The National Defense Authorization Act of 1984 also implemented three rule changes aimed at reducing the cost of military retirement. The first change was to repeal the one-year "look-back" provision, which allowed retirees to base their retired pay either on the pay scale in effect on the date of their retirement or on the immediately preceding pay scale as adjusted for changes in the cost of living, whichever was greater (U.S. Department of Defense, 2005, p. 700). The second change required that retirement payments be rounded down to the next lowest dollar, in accordance with the practice that applied to civil service annuities and Social Security benefits. This change was expected to reduce military retirees' paychecks by no more than $12 per year, but it was estimated to save DoD $9 million annually through 1987 (U.S. Department of Defense, 2005, p. 701). The third change eliminated the practice of rounding fractional YOS greater than six months up to the next highest whole year. Service members were now required to round their YOS down to the next lowest whole month.

Building upon the fifth QRMC report, the DoD submitted proposals in late 1985 to restructure the military retirement system. Congress passed legislation, known as the Military Retirement Reform Act of 1986 (MRRA, also known as "REDUX"), that reflected at least some of the DoD proposals. The most significant change affecting retirement cost implemented by the MRRA was a modification of the multiplier used to calculate retirement benefits. Under the new plan, members received 2 percent per year of service up to 20 YOS, and 3.5 percent per year of service for each year thereafter up to 30 YOS. As a consequence, a retiree with 20 YOS would receive 40 percent of high-three average basic pay (down from 50 percent under the prevailing system), but benefits would reach 75 percent of basic pay at YOS 30, the same percentage as previously. The MRRA also included a change in the cost-of-living adjustment formula: Retired pay during the second-career phase was to be adjusted annually by the CPI minus 1 percent, with a one-time restoration of purchasing power at age 62, followed by CPI minus 1 percent again. The MRRA passed Congress on July 31, 1986, and it applied to persons entering the services after that date.

Not until 2000 did the government conduct another in-depth study of the military retirement system, in this case as part of the Defense Science Board Task Force on Human Resource Strategy (DSB). Like many previous studies, the DSB study cited numerous faults with the prevailing retirement system, calling it "expensive, inefficient, inflexible, and unfair" (DSB, 2000, p. 73). Because of concerns that the MRRA reductions in benefits were unfair, the DSB did not aim to reduce costs. The DSB specifically endorsed fiscal year 2000 legislation ("TRIAD"; see paragraph below) that rolled back the retirement benefit formula to the pre-REDUX formula; i.e., 2.5 percent per year of service, or 50 percent of high-three years of basic pay at 20 YOS.[11]

The National Defense Authorization Act of 2000 made major changes to military pay and benefits. Known as "TRIAD" because of its three, major provisions, the act responded to recruiting and retention difficulties that had appeared in the late 1990s as well as to concerns

---

[11] The task force wrote of the change to the pre-REDUX formula and other pay increases: "These improvements to the military compensation system are an important step in addressing . . . a perception that military pay was falling further . . . behind comparable civilian pay; [and] . . . that the [DoD] had reneged on a public commitment concerning retirement pay and broken faith with the troops" (DSB, 2000, p. 70).

about retirement benefit equity. On the cost side, the act (1) increased basic pay by 4.8 percent and (2) committed to increasing basic pay each year through 2006 by 0.5 percent more than the private-sector Employment Cost Index. On military retirement, service members who had joined after REDUX realized that their retirement benefits would be significantly lower than those who had joined not long before the legislation passed. To address this equity concern, TRIAD gave members the option of reverting to the pre-REDUX formula or staying with REDUX and receiving a $30,000 bonus at 15 YOS for a commitment to stay until 20 YOS.

Equity

Much of the military retirement reform debate has centered on the equity of benefits, where the intent has been to ensure consistency among members with similar service profiles. The chief target of the drive for equity has been the 20-year vesting rule. The problem with the 20-year vesting rule was succinctly described by Professor Herman Leonard of the Kennedy School of Government during congressional committee hearings on the REDUX bill. He said that the system was "an historical accident" that provided benefits to a select few in an "all or nothing" manner (U.S. Congress, 1985, p. 489).[12] A service member who separated (voluntarily or involuntarily) before the 20 YOS mark did not receive a retirement annuity. In the private sector in 1974, the Employee Retirement Income Security Act (ERISA) eliminated such long-tenure vesting rules. Military retirement reformers generally believed that 20 years was too high a hurdle and that there should be some form of benefit—whether a lump-sum separation payment or a "second-career" phase annuity—for those members who failed to vest in the traditional annuity. Many went further by suggesting an earlier vesting point—10 years, for example.

The Hook Commission of 1948 explicitly stated that fairness was a major objective of the retirement system (Advisory Commission on Service Pay, 1948, p. 39). The commission stated that 20-year vesting with payment of an immediate annuity upon retirement was "wholly unreasonable" and not congruent with the objectives of the retirement system (Advisory Commission on Service Pay, 1948, p. 40). However, the commission also recognized that, if the 20-year vesting mark was to be retained to address the superannuation problem, there should be provisions to protect service members who were involuntarily separated before 20 YOS. To address this concern, the commission proposed a new system of severance payments for involuntary separation before 20 YOS. For example, under the commission reforms, involuntary separatees with 10 YOS or more would receive seven and a half months of basic pay plus one and a half months of basic pay for each year of service after 10 YOS, up to a maximum of 2 years of basic pay. (In comparison, today, involuntary nondisability separation pay is computed

---

[12] Professor Leonard's comment belies the fact that the 20-year vesting system emerged as a way to address the problem of superannuation—i.e., preventing an undesirably aged force. The Navy and Marine Corps authorized voluntary retirement of officers after 20 YOS in 1946; and the Army and Air Force followed suit in 1948. See U.S. Department of Defense, 1996, p. 515, for a discussion of the history of the 20-year vesting rule.

as 120 percent of the product of YOS and monthly basic pay). The joint pay board criticized the 20-year vesting provision as well, opting for 10-year vesting with an annuity payable at age 62.

Retirement and compensation reform committees since the Hook Commission have proposed various revisions to the 20-year vesting rule with the goal of making the system fairer. As mentioned before, the first QRMC in 1969 broke new ground by proposing to divide annuity payments into two phases: a first-tier, "second-career" phase, which, contingent upon vesting, would be payable from separation until full retirement age; and a second-tier, "old-age" annuity phase. However, the first QRMC did not alter the 20-year vesting rule and therefore did not attack the major equity concern directly.

The IAC proposed using high-three pay; from an equity perspective, this averaging method would blunt the windfall gains that some members received through the use of a final-pay method. It also criticized the 20-year vesting rule and designed payments for those members who separated between YOS 10 and 19. Service members in this category had the option of an old-age annuity beginning at age 60 or an immediate lump-sum payment.

The RMA listed the correction of inequities as one of its three major objectives (U.S. Defense Manpower Commission, Vol. V, 1976, pp. 1, 53). The bill's proponents argued that it would improve compensation for personnel whose service terminated short of the 20-year retirement eligibility hurdle. Although the 20-year vesting rule remained intact, in agreement with past studies, the RMA accounted for the inequity of the 20-year vesting provision by proposing a system of voluntary and involuntary separation payments and options. As in the IAC proposal, a member who voluntarily separated with 10 to 19 YOS would receive a deferred annuity at age 60 using the standard 2.5 percent formula. Unlike the IAC, the RMA did not contain a lump-sum payment option.

One of the DMC's objectives was to provide members with fair and equitable compensation (U.S. Defense Manpower Commission, Vol. V, 1976, p. 55). It found that 20-year vesting was inequitable and recommended 10-year vesting with an annuity to begin at age 65 (or a reduced, early annuity at age 60).[13]

The PCMC in 1978 contended that fairness should be an important feature of the military retirement system (PCMC, 1978, p. 11). It specifically found that 20-year vesting was unfair to those with significant service less than 20 years in length. To address the problem, the PCMC argued in favor of 10-year vesting in an old-age annuity payable at varying ages depending on length of service. In addition, annuity levels were designed to be comparable to those provided by the federal civil service retirement system.

The fifth QRMC reversed direction and recommended against changing the 20-year vesting rule. A few years later, the MRRA ("REDUX") passed with no change to 20-year vesting. Strong opposition to change came from the military; for example, General Charles Gabriel, then Chief of Staff of the Air Force, testified that he could not support "changing the present 20-year retirement system. That is the one peg point that . . . our people hang their hats on" (U.S. Congress, 1985, p. 489).

---

[13] It is worth noting that approximately one in five military personnel reach 10 YOS, so the DMC's earlier vesting recommendation would not affect 80 percent of service members, unless 10-year vesting changes retention patterns.

The debate over 20-year vesting reignited in 2000 with the DSB report. It took exception to the 20-year vesting system, not so much from an equity perspective as from a force management flexibility angle (see the discussion on force management below). It proposed 5-year vesting, bringing the military in line with many private-sector employers' pension plans.

Not all equity issues centered on 20-year vesting; in 2000, TRIAD raised concerns about benefit equity, but from a different perspective. TRIAD was meant to correct the perceived inequities caused by REDUX more than a decade earlier. The inequity arose from the fact that two service members with slightly different enlistment dates—one before and one after REDUX took effect—would have very different retirement annuity payments. Service members who had joined after REDUX realized that their retirement benefits would be significantly lower than those who had joined not long before the legislation passed. To address this equity concern, TRIAD gave members the option of reverting to the pre-REDUX formula or staying with REDUX and receiving a $30,000 bonus at 15 YOS for a commitment to stay until 20 YOS.

A final equity issue arose with the sixth QRMC and reserve retirement. Here, the proposed change was the addition of a second-career phase of annuity payments. The goal was to bring greater equity between the reserve and regular retirement systems, since the regular retirement system already had the feature of immediate annuity payments after 20 YOS. However, this proposal was not enacted; reserve retirement benefits remained payable at age 60 and not before.

Selective Retention

"Selective retention" refers to the military's objective of retaining certain personnel for career lengths beyond 20 YOS. There is no intrinsic optimality of a 20-year military career, and in many cases the services would prefer member retention rather than separation. Service members with significant value in human capital terms who can still perform their roles beyond 20 YOS without degradation of performance (e.g., physicians) are especially targeted. In past studies of military retirement, there have been many proposals to soften the incentive to retire at 20 YOS.

Under the IAC plan in 1971, the full annuity formula would change to induce greater retention between the 25 and 30 YOS marks (Asch and Warner, 1994b, p. 31). With less than 24 YOS, the multiplier would be the usual 2.5 percent per YOS; after 24 YOS, it would be 3 percent. This "kink" in the formula was designed to increase the incentive to remain in service beyond 20 YOS; at 30 YOS, for example, a retiree would receive 78 percent of pay as opposed to 75 percent under the prevailing system.

The RMA stated that greater selectivity in retaining members beyond 20 YOS was a goal of the legislation (U.S. Defense Manpower Commission, Vol. V, 1976, pp. 1, 53). It also sought to improve retention beyond the 5 YOS mark. The military's chief concern from a force profile perspective was that there were too many service members near the 20-year point and too few junior members; there was a desire to increase the numbers of personnel in the 8 to 12 YOS range, separating out some (possibly with severance payments) but selecting the best to proceed to 20 YOS and beyond (U.S. Congress, 1974, p. 67). Like the IAC proposal before it, the RMA increased the multiplier from 25 to 30 YOS: The factor would increase to 3 percent per YOS, up to a maximum of 78 percent of basic pay.

The DMC found that a 30-year military career, not a 20-year career, was more likely to produce desired skill levels in personnel. The commission proposed a point system that awarded one point for every year of service in a noncombat role, and one and a half points for every year of service in a combat role.[14] To receive an immediate annuity, participants needed thirty points. The DMC thus made a distinction between combat and noncombat roles, changing the hurdle for an immediate annuity to 30 YOS for a person serving exclusively in a noncombat role.

The fifth QRMC suggested a 3 percent multiplier for less than 30 YOS, again reflecting the military's desire for longer service lengths. Congressional testimony on the MRRA/REDUX reflected the concern that the system carried too many personnel to 20 YOS and too few beyond.[15] A few years later, REDUX changed the multiplier to reduce the value of benefits for those with less than 20 YOS and to increase the value to those with more than 20 YOS. Under the REDUX plan, members received 3.5 percent per YOS for each year after 20 YOS up to 30 YOS. A retiree with 30 YOS would therefore receive a maximum of 75 percent of high-three pay. Even though this "increase" was only in relative terms—since members already would receive a maximum of 75 percent under the prevailing system—the obvious incentive effect of this change was to reduce the sharp decline in retention at 20 YOS and induce more-experienced personnel to remain in service for 30 years.

The DSB argued in favor of reverting to the pre-REDUX retirement benefit formula, but at the same time recognized the need for different service lengths and retirement ages, depending on military needs. To accomplish both goals, TRIAD legislation included the option (mentioned above in the discussion of equity) to default to the pre-REDUX formula or receive a bonus with a commitment to stay until the 20 YOS mark. Even though this did not directly affect the 20 to 30 YOS range, in general the changes associated with TRIAD were expected to produce an upward skewness to the pay table, resulting in improved incentives for retention of high-quality personnel (Asch et al., 2002, p. 85).

Civilian Comparability

Defined contribution plans have become commonplace in both private- and government-sector employment, even replacing defined benefit pension plans in some cases. As the military competes for labor with these alternative employers, it has sought ways to offer members some of the features offered by these types of plans. The idea of a contributory retirement plan surfaced as early as 1947 with the Joint Army–Navy Pay Board. Although the Hook Commission recommended that military retirement be noncontributory for "administrative ease," the joint

---

[14] This introduced a different kind of inequity by weighting the contribution of combat service more heavily.

[15] See testimony, for example, of Martin Binkin of the Brookings Institution in U.S. Congress, 1985, p. 489.

pay board suggested a contributory retirement system in which participants would invest in an interest-bearing fund that would vest at 10 YOS, with an annuity payable at age 62.

The Hook Commission's objections to a contributory retirement plan centered on the costs of administering a retirement fund with member contributions. The commission decided that the expenses required to account for contributions to the fund would outweigh any savings from having service members fund part of their own retirement benefits. The Hook Commission observed that such funds are "in reality only bookkeeping entries and the receipts of funds are in fact merged into the general funds of the Treasury and used as such for current expenses" (Advisory Commission on Service Pay, 1948, pp. 40–41). A 1961 study by the University of Michigan backed up the earlier commission findings, arguing that the administrative costs of such a massive fund would probably outweigh any cost savings (U.S. Department of Defense, 2005, pp. 775–776).

The first QRMC in 1967 reversed course on contributory retirement plans, based mainly on an equity argument rather than on a civilian comparability argument. The first QRMC calculated that service member pay would likely be 6.5 percent greater if retirement were contributory. Under this view, the noncontributory system artificially reduced all service members' pay by 6.5 percent, even if many of them were not likely to retire from the military and receive the benefit. For this reason, the first QRMC proposed a 6.5 percent fully vested retirement contribution for "career" members.

In 1978, the PCMC proposed a contributory retirement system. It called for the establishment of a deferred compensation trust fund for each member with more than 5 YOS. The government would make contributions to the fund at rates varying with YOS and give each service member different withdrawal options after vesting at 10 YOS (e.g., lump sum or rollover). The purpose of the deferred compensation fund was to provide added incentive for longer service in the mid-tenure range by making the contribution rate higher in this range than in the initial range of service, as well as to afford service members some financial aid in the transition to civilian life. USRBA modified the PCMC recommendations and went to Congress in 1979. Notably, it abandoned the PCMC's deferred compensation fund in favor of a system that allowed members to borrow against their prospective annuities up to a maximum of 22 months of basic pay. This system was intended to provide compensation for the transition to civilian life—i.e., the second-career phase of retirement. However, USRBA did not receive congressional approval, partly because of Treasury Department opposition to an increase in near-term outlays associated with the change from a defined benefit to a defined contribution system—i.e., the government would have to begin making actual outlays in current years for current-year retirement liabilities (U.S. Department of Defense, 1996, p. 520). The impasse on USRBA led to the subsequent focus on military retirement in the following QRMC.

In the mid-1980s, opinion on a contributory retirement plan for the military swung again, with the fifth QRMC coming down against the idea, citing modeling exercises that showed a decrease in enlisted career force strengths if a change to a contributory plan was made (U.S. Department of Defense, Vol. I, 1984, p. X-5).[16] In the 1990s, retirement studies began to revive the defined contribution concept and the offering of earlier vesting of those contribu-

---

[16] The assumption of relatively low contribution rates might have affected the outcome of the modeling exercises.

tions. For example, in 1998, RAND Corporation proposed a contributory plan component modeled after the Federal Employees Retirement System that featured vesting at 3 YOS, with employer matching contributions of up to 5 percent of basic pay (Asch, Johnson, and Warner, 1998, p. xii). In 1999, the Armed Services committees of the House and Senate recommended a tax-deferred savings plan for military service members, with the goal of improving their financial security. In 2000, the DSB recommended benefit portability through a 401(k)-type option similar to the Federal Employee Thrift Savings Plan (TSP).

After years of debate, the National Defense Authorization Act of 2000 extended participation in the TSP to military personnel, giving service members a true defined contribution retirement benefit.[17] Service members can contribute from 1 to 9 percent of basic pay before taxes to their accounts, and up to 100 percent of any incentive or special pays, subject to Internal Revenue Service limits. There are generally no matching employer contributions; however, the act authorized the Secretary concerned to make TSP contributions if the member is serving in a critical skill and agrees to continued service. By adopting the TSP for military service members, the armed forces joined a growing list of private-sector employers at the turn of the 21st century who were placing greater emphasis on defined contribution plans over traditional pension plans. Participation among service members ranged from 16 percent of Army personnel to 34 percent of Navy personnel as of 2004 (U.S. Department of Defense, 2005, pp. 941).

Force Management Flexibility

Perhaps more than any other objective, force management flexibility has guided calls for military retirement reform.[18] The military's principal concern with respect to pay and benefits is force readiness—primarily, do the incentives imbedded in the compensation system deliver desired force structure profiles through optimal separation and retention? Although cost and equity concerns grow and wane through the history of military retirement reform, force management flexibility remains a paramount goal to the military. In the context of retirement reform, this goal takes the form of two, key issues: (1) providing benefits for members serving less than 20 years (see the discussions on equity and selective retention, above), and (2) providing separation incentives that vary by skill.

The Hook Commission recognized that "attrition is an unfortunate necessity if the Military Services are to be kept vital" (Advisory Commission on Service Pay, 1948, p. 44). In other words, the "up-or-out" nature of military promotions would necessitate involuntary separations. It also stated that the primary objective of its review of retirement pay was to address the superannuation problem, and that the fundamental rationale for a retirement plan was to keep the Armed Forces "alert and vigorous" (Advisory Commission on Service Pay, 1948, p. 39). As one way of achieving these ends, the commission recommended retirement pay formu-

---

[17] The 2001 National Defense Authorization Act modified the effective date provision.

[18] As a point of comparison, it should be noted that resistance to military retirement system reform has not always been motivated by force management concerns.

las for involuntary separation. These would address equity concerns, ensuring that members with long lengths of service would not be left entirely without compensation. However, they would also aid the military in shaping the force profile by softening the impact of necessary separations.

The RMA aimed to provide an improved personnel management tool to aid DoD in attaining a preferred experience distribution among those in the active force (U.S. Defense Manpower Commission, Vol. V, 1976, pp. 1, 53). As stated above, there were deemed to be too many long-tenured (about 20 YOS) service members and too few junior members with mid-tenure service (8 to 12 YOS). In addition to the incentives for retention beyond 20 YOS, the RMA also proposed a system of voluntary and involuntary separation payments and options. A member with 10 YOS could receive a deferred annuity beginning at age 60 under the RMA plan.

As previously mentioned, the DMC proposed a point system for the receipt of annuity benefits that made a distinction between combat and noncombat roles. Thirty points were required to receive the immediate annuity, but the DMC effectively made deferred separation pay possible by allowing those who had 10 points, but less than 30, eligible to receive an old-age annuity. Under the DMC proposal, the services would have a relatively blunt tool to manage the force by discriminating on the basis of combat and noncombat roles.

The PCMC found that the 20-year vesting rule made it difficult to separate ineffective personnel and stated that force management was therefore a primary issue that needed to be addressed (PCMC, 1978, p. 11). It is notable that the PCMC listed force management as only one of several motivations in redesigning military retirement. In fact, the commission did not view retirement as the principal lever of force structure, instead taking the position that cost savings from the retirement system should be reallocated to targeted types of active pay (bonuses and special pays) to induce retention and reenlistment (PCMC, 1978, p. 4, and Asch and Warner, 1994b, p. 34). Against this backdrop, the PCMC stated that an effective military retirement program should assist in manning the force—i.e., by providing incentives to stay in military service, but not to the extent that involuntary separation would cause undue economic hardship (PCMC, 1978, pp. 61–62). The commission believed that 20-year vesting was inequitable and detrimental to force flexibility since it made managers reluctant to separate ineffective personnel approaching retirement eligibility. The commission recommended 10-year vesting with eligibility for an old-age annuity beginning at varying ages depending on YOS, as well as severance pay for those who are involuntarily terminated. When the modified recommendations of the PCMC—in the form of USRBA—went before Congress, the armed forces questioned the plan's effect on force structure and retention (Asch and Warner, 1994b, p. 35).

When MRRA/REDUX went before Congress, the services argued that radical change to military retirement—for example, by changing 20-year vesting—could negatively affect force structure. Twenty-year vesting did not change with the legislation, and the bill did not include severance pay for those separating before 20 YOS.

Military retirement became a key instrument of flexible force management in the early 1990s as the services began to draw down their forces. Early retirement authority was granted to the services with the National Defense Authorization Act of 1993. This legislation specified that service members with between 15 and 20 YOS could apply for early retirement to assist the force drawdown. The authority was originally given from 1992 until 1995, but it was later extended to 1999. The early retirement multiplier was calculated as the pre-REDUX multiplier (i.e., 2.5 percent per year of service), minus 1 percent per year of service less than 20 years.[19] Congress noted that early retirement programs had been successful in the past for the 6- to 15-YOS range, and that it was expected to be similarly useful in the 15- to 20-YOS range for the drawdown of the 1990s (U.S. Department of Defense, 2005, p. 711).

The DSB called military retirement a "one-size-fits-all" program that was inflexible across different branches, ranks, and experience levels (DSB, 2000, p. 73). Furthermore, it took exception to the 20-year vesting system. The DSB study pointed out that the 20-year system caused too many members to get promoted to O-4 rank, which typically occurs around YOS 10 to 12; the system essentially guaranteed keeping personnel on board for 20 years once reaching this rank, even though there may be more personnel than available billets in the higher-rank range. As a result, personnel had to be rotated through assignments quickly to keep promotions on pace, which in turn hurt skill development and force readiness.[20] The DSB proposed separation pay in the form of early annuity or lump-sum payments, for which the timing of the first payment could be varied by skill—i.e., early payments for those skills in which the military wanted to increase separations, and later (or no) payments for those skills in which the military wanted to increase retention.

Table 1 summarizes and compares some of the major retirement reform proposals since 1969.

Reserve Retirement Reform

The reserve forces retirement system has also been the subject of reform proposals over the years. Much like the regular retirement system, the focus of reform has often centered on cost reduction. The Reserve Compensation System Study of 1978 (RCSS) attempted to address several perceived problems. It found the reserve retirement system to be too costly, and it recommended either reducing reserve retirement annuities by 20 percent to 35 percent or scrapping the reserve retirement program entirely (U.S. Department of Defense, Executive Summary, 2005, pp. 122–123). The reserve system changed its measure of pay used in the computation of benefits in 1980. Legislation that year established the average of the highest three years of basic pay (as opposed to final basic pay) as the measure to be used for all those entering the reserves on or after September 8, 1980. The sixth QRMC in 1988, which focused on reserve pay and benefits, parted ways with the RCSS and recommended not only maintaining the reserve retirement system, but also extending it to include a second-career annuity phase option. The two-tiered system, although more costly in the short run, would provide substantial cost savings in the long run because the near-term increase in outlays from the retirement

---

[19] The early retirement multiplier was actually calculated on a monthly basis, so that fractional YOS became possible.

[20] As an aside, observers have pointed out that pressure for fast rotation would be reduced if some personnel were on a technical track rather than a general officer or top enlisted-grade track.

Table 1
Comparison of Retirement Reform Proposals
(for an E-8 retiring with 20 YOS at age 42)

Commission/ Legislation	Vesting Rule (YOS)	Age Payments Begin	Multiplier	Pay Basis	Monthly Annuity Amount	Comments
1st QRMC (1967)	20	42 (2C); 62 (OA)	24% (2C); 33% (OA)	Final salary	$1,472 (2C); $2,025 (OA)	Proposed a contributory system. SS offset
IAC (1971)	20	42 (2C); 60 (OA)	14% (2C); 50% (OA)	Highest 3 years of average basic pay	$579 (2C); $2,067 (OA)	Multiplier reduced by 2% per year of service under age 60 at time of retirement; full multiplier restored at age 60. SS offset
RMA (1974)	20	42 (2C); 52 (OA)	35% (2C); 50% (OA)	Highest 1 year of average basic pay	$1,472 (2C); $2,103 (OA)	2C annuity reduced by 15%; full annuity restored at time 30 YOS would have been completed. SS offset
DMC (1976)	10	65 (norm) 60 (early)	50%	Highest 3 years of average basic pay	$2,067	Immediate annuity if 30 retirement points earned (1.5 points/year of service for combat, 1.0/year of service for noncombat). No SS offset
PCMC/Zwick (1978)	10	60 (at 20 YOS); depends on YOS	50%	Highest 3 years of average basic pay	$2,067	Offered stepped "transition" benefits. SS offset
USRBA (1979)	10	42 (2C); 60 (OA)	37.5% (2C); 55% (OA)	Highest 2 years of average basic pay	$1,557 (2C); $2,284 (OA)	SS offset
REDUX (1986) (current plan[a])	20	42 (2C); 62 (OA)	40% (2C); 50% (OA)	Highest 3 years of average basic pay	$1,653 (2C); $2,067 (OA)	Receive a $30,000 Career Status Bonus at 15 YOS in exchange for reduced multiplier before age 62. SS offset. Did not fully protect from inflation: CPI – 1 during 2C phase, with a one-time cost-of-living adjustment restoration at age 62, then CPI – 1 increases thereafter

NOTES: 2C = second-career phase of retirement; OA = old-age phase of retirement; SS = Social Security. Multiplier is shown as a product of percentage of pay and YOS. Age Payments Begin assumes the participant retires with 20 YOS at age 42. Pay Basis for the first QRMC was final salary; for the purpose of the calculation of the first QRMC Monthly Annuity Amount, estimated 2006 regular military compensation for an E-8 with 20 YOS is used (approximately $73,618). Monthly Annuity Amount is calculated using the estimated January 2006 monthly basic pay rate for an E-8 with 20 YOS ($4,206.80); all amounts are in 2006 dollars.

[a] There are also two grandfathered retirement plans; see the text for details.

fund (to pay for the early annuities) would be offset by the lower accrual payments made by the DoD into the trust.

Force management flexibility concerns also arose in studies of the reserve retirement system. At the time of the RCSS in 1978, during the post–Vietnam War period, the key manpower concerns of the military were recruiting and early attrition problems, not retention problems. As a result, the RCSS proposed a greater emphasis on current pay rather than on forms of deferred compensation such as retirement.

Legislation in 1980 affected reserve force structure. A distinction was made between those who separated and entered the "retired reserve" and those who were discharged completely from the reserves. Those who joined the retired reserve would have the average pay of their highest three years computed using the pay scale for those years immediately preceding normal retirement at age 60. Those who left the reserves entirely would have the average pay of their highest three years computed using the pay scale for those years immediately preceding their date of separation. Thus, the reserve retirement system added a strong financial incentive to remain a "gray area" retiree, who could be recalled to active duty (Gordon, 2002, p. 47). It also provided an incentive for any reservist who qualified for retirement to consider leaving the reserves and becoming a retired reserve member rather than continuing to occupy a position and clog promotion pathways in the selected reserves.

The sixth QRMC stated that its principal objective was to "determine the extent to which the current reserve retirement system effectively supports service and reserve component manpower objectives and policies, and aid in achieving desired manpower force structures" (U.S. Department of Defense, Executive Summary, 2005, p. 120). It cited the effects of the retirement system on force structure as a major area of review. The sixth QRMC openly questioned whether the reserve retirement system was an effective force-shaping tool when the ratio of officers to enlisted personnel retiring from the reserve components was three to one.[21] Against this background, the sixth QRMC made a substantial set of recommendations on reserve retirement (see Table 2). These included adopting a two-tiered retirement system, with the option to receive an early annuity immediately upon separation conditional on eligibility; and changing the point system used to determine years of creditable service—specifically, increasing the annual cap on inactive duty training points from 60 to 75.[22] The analyses of the sixth QRMC concluded that a reserve retirement system was critical to providing a cost-effective means for incentives for long tenures.[23] Without the benefit, the reserves would lose valuable experience as a result of attrition. Furthermore, in addition to the old-age annuity, some individuals would be eligible for an early annuity in the time between separation and age 62 that would be based on a reduced-point formula. This recommendation was believed to offer several advantages and benefits. Foremost among them was that an early annuity offered the incentive to remain in the reserves; the annuity would represent an amount large enough to support reserve manpower requirements without luring away regular, active-duty personnel.

---

[21] However, it should be noted that even in the regular military there is a higher flow of officers than enlisted personnel to retirement.

[22] The annual cap on inactive duty training points now stands at 90.

[23] The sixth QRMC admitted that it would be possible to replace reserve retirement with current compensation, but it based its conclusion of the cost-effectiveness of the former over the latter on an analysis that included training and accession costs. In its view, the costly loss of experienced reservists due to the elimination of the reserve retirement system would outweigh the savings of plan elimination. See U.S. Department of Defense, Executive Summary, 2005, p. 123.

Table 2
Sixth QRMC Reserve Retirement Alternatives

Alternative	Element	Estimated Effect	Recom-mended
1. Eliminate current system. Replace with pay increases	Would require average after-tax pay increase of 10% to 17% to hold accession rates constant	Increased cost Favorable separation of long-service personnel Mid-career retention problems	No
2. Reduce the retirement benefit	Would reduce value of reserve retirement benefit by 20%	Decreased normal cost Increased accession requirements, initial entry training costs Unfavorable separation of long-service personnel	No
3. Offer early retirement annuity	Reduced, actuarially neutral early annuity	Decreased retention among those with most retirement credit points	No
4. Offer two-tier early annuity option	Offer early annuity at 20 YOS with second-tier annuity to begin at age 62	Favorable retention of mid-career personnel and favorable separation of long-service personnel Small decrease in accession requirements Short-term increase and long-term decrease in cost	Yes

The reserve retirement system was also used as a force management tool in the 1990s drawdown. Long-tenured reservists were in relatively strong supply, and so to facilitate the drawdown, the National Defense Authorization Act of 1993 instituted two temporary force management tools: an immediate annuity for members with 20 YOS, but not yet age 60, and a voluntary early retirement option for reservists with between 15 and 20 YOS. Like the early retirement authority for the regular military, these changes were seen as temporary force management instruments and were scheduled to be revoked once an appropriate force reduction had taken place.[24]

Recently, there has been renewed interest in reforming the reserve retirement system. Reserve deployments have increased substantially in recent years as the reserves have taken on an expanded role in the nation's defense strategy. Several pieces of legislation specifically centered on the reserve retirement system have been introduced in the latest session of Congress.[25] They include the following:

- H.R. 331—providing an immediate annuity to eligible reservists.
- H.R. 742—reducing annuity payout age from 60 to 55, with no reduction in annuity amount.
- S. 1000—revising age and eligibility requirements on a sliding scale: at 20 YOS, retire at age 60; at 22 YOS, retire at age 59; up to 34 YOS, retire at age 53.

---

[24] The authority originally lasted until 1995 but was later extended to 1999.

[25] At the time this report was originally written—2003.

- S. 1035 (companion legislation to H.R. 742)—reducing annuity payout age from 60 to 55, with no reduction in annuity amount.

Much of the motivation for these proposals is the perceived inequity between the regular system, which pays an immediate annuity, and the reserve system, which does not. The increasing burden of national defense being placed on the reserves has made reserve retirement reform a more pressing policy issue.

Conclusion

The military retirement system has remained much the same for the past 60 years. Major elements of the system—e.g., 20-year vesting and the 2.5 percent multiplier—have demonstrated remarkable resilience. The serial QRMC and other commissioned studies have kept alive calls for reform. Not surprisingly, many of the past studies have reached similar conclusions. Their recommendations can be broadly grouped into the five categories discussed in this memorandum: cost, equity, selective retention, civilian comparability, and force management flexibility.

On cost, studies have generally concluded that the military retirement system is too expensive. Because it pays an immediate annuity regardless of age, benefit payment streams are usually longer, driving up the cost of the system. To address this problem, the studies have typically recommended a two-tier retirement system in which a reduced benefit amount is paid in the first-tier or second-career phase, and a "restored" benefit is paid at a later date during the second-tier, old-age annuity phase.

Fairness has motivated military retirement reform to some extent as well. Much of the discussion of equity has focused on the 20-year vesting rule, which rewards the relatively small subset of military personnel who remain in service to that point. Reform proposals have often recommended earlier vesting—usually 10 years—with an old age annuity to be paid at a later date. Some studies have addressed the equity issue by proposing the adoption of severance payments for those who are involuntarily separated.

Another common thread in past retirement studies has been the proposal to include a defined contribution plan in the military retirement system, either by replacing the defined benefit plan or in addition to it. Civilian comparability is the objective of these proposals; reformers have argued that such a plan would make military compensation more competitive with the private sector and offer features that service members demand. This is one area of military retirement system reform that has experienced dramatic change recently: The armed forces have adopted a defined contribution plan based on the federal employees' TSP.

Military retirement studies have universally acknowledged that the retirement benefit plays a key role in providing retention and separation incentives. Although many of these studies also suggest that retirement can be a blunt instrument for shaping the force, they recognize the need for careful analysis of the effects of changes in the system on force structure. The military's personnel concerns have varied over time, ranging from aging populations to diminishing ranks of mid-career service members. For this reason, there has been a wide array of recommendations in past studies to address the prevailing manpower problem of the day. For example, studies and legislation such as IAC (1971), REDUX (1986), and TRIAD (2000) have attempted to increase retention of selected personnel beyond 20 YOS by altering the benefit formula to increase the rate of growth in benefits in this range.

Historically, reserve retirement has received much less attention than the regular retirement system, although there has been a recent increase in activity due to the expanded role of the reserves in the military's defense strategy. The provision of an immediate, second-career phase annuity for reservists—or, at a minimum, an earlier annuity option—has been the primary focus of recent reform efforts. The motivating argument is that the reserve forces are playing a role that is increasingly similar to the regular forces, and therefore reservists should enjoy similar retirement benefits.

By one estimate, between fiscal years 1995 and 2005, total compensation costs for current and former military personnel increased by almost 60 percent. The military retirement benefit remains a significant portion of these costs, and every change to accessions, retention, and basic pay today will have a future effect on pension expenditures. Cost alone is reason enough to analyze the current retirement system, and reform proposals of the past have focused carefully on cost. However, as the military's mission evolves over time, it is also important to consider the sometimes subtle incentive effects that the retirement system has on service member behavior. Beyond considerations of cost, reform of the military retirement system necessarily involves ramifications for force structure and operational readiness.

Bibliography

Advisory Commission on Service Pay, *Career Compensation for the Uniformed Forces, A Report and Recommendation for the Secretary of Defense,* Washington, D.C., December 1948.

Asch, Beth J., James Hosek, Jeremy Arkes, C. Christine Fair, Jennifer Sharp, and Mark E. Totten, *Military Recruiting and Retention After the Fiscal Year 2000 Military Pay Legislation,* Santa Monica, Calif.: RAND Corporation, MR-1532-OSD, 2002.

Asch, Beth J., Richard Johnson, and John T. Warner, *Reforming the Military Retirement System,* Santa Monica, Calif.: RAND Corporation, MR-748-OSD, 1998.

Asch, Beth J., and John T. Warner, *A Policy Analysis of Alternative Military Retirement Systems,* Santa Monica, Calif.: RAND Corporation, MR-465-OSD, 1994a.

———, *A Theory of Military Compensation and Personnel Policy,* Santa Monica, Calif.: RAND Corporation, MR-439-OSD, 1994b.

DSB—*see U.S. Defense Science Board Task Force on Human Resource Strategy.*

Gordon, Sol, *Reserve Forces Almanac,* Washington, D.C.: Uniformed Services Almanac, Inc., 2002.

PCMC—*see U.S. President's Commission on Military Compensation.*

U.S. Congress, 99th Congress, 1st Sess., Department of Defense Authorization of Appropriations for Fiscal Year 1986 and Oversight of Previously Authorized Programs Before the Committee on Armed Services, Washington, D.C.: U.S. Government Printing Office, H.R. 1872, 1985.

U.S. Congress, 93rd Congress, 2nd Sess., Uniformed Services Retirement Act and H.R. 14081 and Other Recomputation Bills : Hearings Before Subcommittee No. 4 of the Committee on Armed Services, Washington, D.C.: U.S. Government Printing Office, H.R. 12505, 1974.

U.S. Defense Manpower Commission, *Defense Manpower Commission Staff Studies and Supporting Papers, Volumes I–V,* Washington, D.C.: U.S. Government Printing Office (GPO), 1976.

U.S. Defense Science Board Task Force on Human Resource Strategy (DSB), *Defense Science Board Task Force on Human Resources Strategy,* Washington, D.C.: U.S. GPO, 2000.

U.S. Department of Defense, *Military Compensation Background Papers: Compensation Elements and Related Manpower Cost Items, Their Purposes and Legislative Backgrounds, 5th ed.,* Washington, D.C.: U.S. GPO, September 1996.

———, *Military Compensation Background Papers: Compensation Elements and Related Manpower Cost Items, Their Purposes and Legislative Backgrounds, 6th ed.,* Washington, D.C.: U.S. GPO, May 2005.

———, *Fifth Quadrennial Review of Military Compensation,* Washington, D.C.: U.S. GPO, 1984.

————, *Sixth Quadrennial Review of Military Compensation,* Washington, D.C.: U.S. GPO, 1988.

U.S. President's Commission on Military Compensation (PCMC), *Report of the President's Commission on Military Compensation,* Washington, D.C.: U.S. GPO, 1978.